dancing on all fours

mark hallman

no rhyme   *no reason*

Published by Toth Press
315 South 20th Street
San José, CA 95116

Some pieces appeared previously in the following
publications:
*Ball Magazine; Bay Windows; Black Sheets; The Evergreen
Chronicles; Exquisite Corpse; Gents, Bad Boys, and
Barbarians; Iris; Joey and the Black Boots; Just Add Water;
Kudzu; New Beginnings; The New Voice of Nebraska; Plump
Testicles; Salome; Sand River Journal; Sex and Spirit; Shared
Affections; Snail Tracks; So it goes ...; Utterants; White Crane
Newsletter; Wilde Oaks; 1995 Poet's Market*

The following are either trademarks, registered trademarks, or
service marks of their respective companies:
*Bic, Burger King, Compound W, Costco, Demerol, El Dorado,
Guinness, Joy, Macy's, Pampers, Valium, Wendy's, Wheel of
Fortune*

Cover art and design by Mike Bromberg/Design by Mike
Cover photo by David Bolduc

ISBN 0-9646610-5-5

appreciation to the following for advice, inspiration, and endurance of my caprice (including the ones who can't take it any longer)

Agnes
David
Eric
Greg
Joe
John
Craig
VCR

dancing on all fours

animals

lay guinea pigs or chickens
on their backs   gently
stroke their bellies
they quickly fall
asleep

with men
something completely different happens

disco concertino

notes fly past
tiny angels buffeted on happy helium
wings beating the speed of hummingbirds'
in gusts that pitch little bodies
through the air at odd angles

their laughter and trilling voices
bounce off our shiny white smiles

    put a twitch in our heels

imagine

if hitler did it all
with a solitary ball
think what newt might do
if he has a set of two

Daddy's dreamboy

a fairly disheveled marine with no sleep under his belt
slunk from my house at six on a sunday morning
    promising to call   the usual words
    a novice   not a problem
just he'd never admit
how much he had enjoyed himself

so i thought   he appeared at my door monday evening
      shoes shining   my favorite colors
insisting   despite my obligatory protestations
   on dinner first   a soldier's treat
     the son of my father's dreams

jumper cables

burn scars on my temples
are the only memories left
of the interval that started
when the market dropped
and ended once i could no longer
remember the specifics of your odor

i still awaken saturdays
with the cool of eucalyptus
on my tongue

inside karen carpenter's coffin

vocal cords lie silent
in specks of dust around your neckbone
finally the figure you wanted to be

you went clean   not a liz

i heard you today in the elevator
after i left the IRS office
young lady humming "close to you"
she could've been your granddaughter

head buzzed bare down the middle
and on the sides   remaining spikes
    pink   green   firework drizzle

boots   good condition   not new

she popped a blister of gum on beat
didn't let braces keep her from
tossing me a follow-through smile
monica seles couldn't have done it slicker

normal girl

summer vacation

i hooked the kids
to high-nutrition i-vees

plus a daily drop of anesthesia

beauty

house of firemen
scrubbing their truck
on a sunny day

vials of morphine

easy lay   prey   loses its way
in my maze of caustic cubism

i force its escape
into hands that don't require
analysis before action

next one   snagged   to eat the pain

serious business

late at night i stretch a leg
down between the sheets
to the foot of the bed
where Agnes sleeps
lightly rub a big toe up   down
her soft furry belly

muffled "grrr!"
                    i know i better quit

toward utah at speed limit

those cycling heels
your cycling heels
please
stop them

the electricity flowing through charlie's veins
is beyond our power now

we did what we could
again and again
but you can't stop it

ragweed either dies or blooms
and then dies

don't turn the car around
none of these exits will take you back
or keep us from going where we will

charlie wouldn't have tried to save us
that's the way things are
among people like us

      we do and we keep going
     we don't fool ourselves with hope
   so quickly we'd harden
pillars of salt

under the floor of ziggurat 3

the sign said
no one enter the hole
    it stood open
as if jesus had spitefully
thrown aside the metal grille

my flashlight a bic lighter
mostly used to ignite weed
and enhance perception
now neither

all surfaces were free of right angles
as well as the shadows they release

the allure leaned proud
with shoulder blades cutting
into the arch toward the ceiling

a thousand years and variations
in skin had changed nothing

normalcy

infant of centuries
of inbreeding

coffee cups

flowers	bears	dali	bees
kisses	grapes	mickey	geese
candy	stripes	wooly	goats
peking	ducks	eating	oats
comets	tots	apples	trains
kittens	frogs	dogs andplanes	
buddhas	feet	pots of	gold
week-old	brew	acrid	mold

all the dead miss americas

revert to dust
as their heels   gowns   crowns
collect more in the attics
of their grandchildren

fresh milk

straight from the teat
into my mouth

no bucket   supermarket   plastic container
to inflate the price

your hand grabs high
     fingers squeeze low
in sequence

the white stream strikes a dimple
then home between the lips

susie snorts   swishes her tail

truth is a calico cat

it purrs   it scratches
it's a sex-linked trait

rush

a man with hot air
in his balls

fahrenheitfirefahrenheitfrost

foliage on this twisted tree cycles color
every quarter-second
    green   red   blue   yellow
                    black   white

best i can do is a feeble juggle
    own up to the fact
        i'm a twirler in the air

        planet x holds orbit
        planet y drops closer to the sun
            each season handing off the baton
            faster than the preceding

i'm the one who put myself out to pasture
    the one who'll have to bring me back
grass doesn't grow in hell or winter

        the price of purity also its poison

plump little chicken in her blue overalls

she's such an ugly little girl   big-boned
    fat cheeks   overweight at four   for life
    slitty eyes with nothing shining through
    but ego and greed   things it's good she's got
before long   she's going to feel
what it's like to watch the pretty little girls
get the good seats and best responses
    she'll get a lasting taste of being
ignored and laboriously tolerated   that's
what she gets for having that long spiny nose
stubby chubby fingers   pasty spotty skin
hair that's going to baffle every permanent
that goes into it (a lot will go into it)
    she'll have to learn to shake off what mother
hasn't let her see   mother keeps her home
away from other children   tells her every
fifteen minutes what a pretty little girl she is
       mother knows in every part of her head
        that her little girl
         is just as ugly as an ugly little girl can be

politics

     one day   you're the pig's potato
the next   falling out the other end

landfill

i used to have trouble throwing away old belongings
then i learned
to think of them
as people

stale shampoo

long hair lies on the kitchen floor
shaved away
you sound asleep numb

i like you now
bald and bristly

the irritating smiles
swept out with the locks

new york city

mecca
of the most intelligent
and ambitious of

              idiots

depression

what gods give the me's
to keep us from destroying
your universe

real women who look like drag queens

they're all over the place at work
    the hallways   the cafeteria   the cubicle next to me
they buy makeup at costco by the tubful
they have no waists to speak of   just hyped-up cheek bones
i dread conversations with them   they say outrageous things
in large voices that whoop and resonate through doors
recently closed   with clear intent
      their ping pong paddle hands
      and broomstick arms flit and flap
      in unnecessary emphasis of what they're saying
          buzzards shooing flies from summer aardvark
burning butts hang from painted fingers
that tap big bony hips during break
                    thumps of impatience
lipstick the color of national flags
hair changes color and shape in sudden rushes
    one new `do walks in monday   friday offers
a peck   long feet carry them
from this cup of coffee to the next
lip prints on pinkish porcelain

        oh   the relentless search for a real man

rest stop

semi trucks parked side-by-side
snag my interest
meat-hooks into a carcass of beef
anxious to be tossed on a metal table
      slowly quartered
saws buzzing

scavenger scavenged

his eyes locked on me
with the fierceness
of a vulture's on fresh carrion

next morning
he was the one
missing a few tail feathers

I probably would've made a good little nazi

at the age of eight   I lassoed sister with baling twine
tethered her spread-eagle to azalea bushes
tickled bare feet until the screams of anguish
brought our parents running

in seventh grade I clashed heads with the science teacher
over the accuracy of a detail
regarding the male anatomy
     that night I wished a curse on him
     by the end of the decade   dead
     cancer of the regenerative organs   they said

ten years on I courted a woman so effectively
she beseeched me to marry her   promising some of daddy's
money
"honey"   I replied   "you're a great cook
          there's just one problem
you've got the wrong equipment   down there"

tonight I wrapped my lover in long strips of texas leather
transforming him into an oversized babe
in black swaddling clothes
a big old moses writhing in ecstasy from my manipulations
"please!"   he whimpered   almost an hour "finish me off!"
          groans in the background   I called Mother
     his

hymnal

sorry sunday
the religion served up
bland and stale as the communion bread
shed from the hide of the preacher
his meanness of face and torque of tongue
pure distillate of the congregational vinegar

town of cousins

nothing unlike us was to be found
forty miles
or several hundred years
our options so progressively thinned
by vehement history and our own stubborn doing
    we had little to strive for
other than what we'd inherited
the carapace molted by each generation
crowded in under the one before it
stifling us further
a world fated to bear
unsalvageable crazies   misfits of niche
       and voices that skittered along linings
of thickening skulls

where the trout don't talk

i got several strikes tonight
three i hooked easily
pulled into the boat
nice ones

an hour later
they didn't seem worth the trouble

i tossed them back
put away my tackle
in exchange for my favorite spot
where i dived into a pool
of ten-minute feeders who didn't care
about names or addresses
   and became one myself

best buddy

piss down the throat
quiet hours of dining at risk
careless cruising on creaking floors
a hand at untampered fare
   or   in his absence
home alone in ones or twos
the lack of plan the point of it all

longer

fifteen centuries of waiting
in streams of guileless rumor
        i watch for those i know
long overdue
promise fading
no reason to sink or fly
        moment coming soon
to discard the purpose
concede to sleep

how history is made

    some people are more about
where they're going than where
they come from
    you better not try mixing
the two   particularly in love
the ultimate genetic mutation
    people with eyes on the
future are always underway
they rush forward continuously
sloughing off anything older
than the present
    people of the past
snap it up   have it refinished

conversations during intimacy   #16

    jesus! aren't you tired yet
no   i wanna go another round
    again   you must've done nothing but sleep all day
no   i was over at rick's till three
   what were you doing there
what we're doing here

sex with crazy people

the best sex i've ever had has been with crazy people
they don't care what they do or what you do
they don't have to   they're crazy
there's nothing to stop them
they like tearing off the skin
   put it back on   inside out
they like biting to the bone with eyes too happy
   let little squeals of pain
     leak through ears
   they laugh where most would cry
   compliment what most would curse
   sex with crazy people is dangerous
the only kind i want

balls

kids next door knock their ball into my backyard   come
to get it   check with me first   my dogs might tear out
after them

sometimes i answer the bell   tell them to go ahead   tell
them i've locked the dogs inside

other times i tiptoe to the rear window

                      to see what happens

no sweat

the best
bed partners
i've ever had
never set foot
in a gym

hundreds of dollars later

i should've known better
than wager so much time
on a pretty boy of such dubious potential
        having learned by damage
their only real asset is to look good on film

but in a world ruled by double chins
garish watches   and   size forty-four waists
that's sometimes enough

eye on my wallet

dropping names
won't pay your bills

dropping drawers
might

jaded

the screen offers the best porn in town
the ceiling the sleaziest of slings
the backroom beckons with more than darkness

you play pinball

image

all these perfect little gym bodies!
    somebody   please take them to the city dump
bring me back a torn-seat cane chair
i can stick a potted plant in
and tell everybody i picked it up
south of market
for only four hundred ninety-five dollars
and they'll believe me!

bar experience

men fresh out of jail
rarely complain
when beds offer little
but unbroken sleep

poetry metric

the words of the guy who won
the last four slam competitions
down at the coffee shop
didn't fare so well
once rendered in braille

now successful

and the smile's the same
as when you sold it
on the street

conversations during intimacy   #14

    my brother's gay   you want me to introduce you
he anything like you
    we look alike   but he's gay
what are you
    straight
what about what we just did
    i only do that every now and then

dew

in forty-five years the town
had seen twenty-eight preachers
remembered only one

   the cool warming smile
scattered so wide
among the blossoms of youth

prey

seeing the things
those men wanted to do to you
I saved you
by taking you home
and doing them myself

porking

ham on sale   i brought home a twenty-pounder
ate a few chunks   let my dogs (tiny things)
have at it until their sides were sagging
     leaving a good fifteen pounds
which i sliced up   ran through the food processor
          the outcome   nearly two gallons of ham puree

no plans for the evening
i drew up a tub of hot water   took off my clothes
poured in the puree   immersed myself
after soaking more than an hour   got out
          (water cooling   fat congealing)
dried off as best i could   went to bed

at three   i woke from a nightmare that cast me
as a block of salt
lapped by the rough tongues of holstein cattle

just the dogs   one licking my leg   the other my neck
eyes closed to slits   faces aglow
          the contentment of piglets nursing

conversations during intimacy   #6

you like big dicks
doesn't matter
what about mine
what about it
is it big
big enough
i mean   compared to others
above average
a guy gave me a ride the other day
pulled out his dick   wanted me
to go down on him   said he'd give me
thirty dollars
you do it
no
how come
his dick scared me   it was this big
around and this long   soft
so
he was a big dude too   guys like that
can really mess you up if they get rough
i wouldn't know

dead time man

"this is what had you plugged up"
the sewer prole said as he dangled
the lynched facecloth from a yellow-gloved hand
pulling my attention to a scaffolded frame
an articulated light-pole
tattoos slithering up under soiled arm-sleeves
carrot nose off-center on a kangaroo face
honky-tonk denizen   blue-collar   hang-dog eyes
a mouth that didn't bother with grinning
spaghetti-shorn hazelnut strings
parted somewhere from the back
caked shoes
the kind who spoke of "the ol' lady"
    asked to wash up in the bathroom
emerging five minutes later
in thread-bare boxers that
rendered precise   distinct outlines
saying with unstudied matter-of-factness
        having spotted truth in my venal pupils
    his mind   thankfully   devoid of cutesy
"got an hour to kill"

bones on paper

skulls georgia o'keeffe
immortalized for city apartments
gaze down next door
on a family that barbecues weekends
and goes to matinees with the kids
occasionally leaving Daddy at home
with me to interpret the reality
behind the pictures

on the stool at the end of the bar

he had hands with blood long down the drain
i could sense it
from the way his eyes took in everything
without creasing a muscle
instinct not to drip a drop
wait   for precisely the right moment

white collar crimes

construction workers eating alone
in the company cafeteria
    such good little boys
ready to do
whatever I tell them

you called Her "Gladys"

a few things you should know

    the spot you occupied all night long   it belongs to Her

    my feel for human nature isn't the best in the world

    Agnes   this little canine abacus who knows not only
    Her name but yours as well   has never been wrong

headless chickens

the woman who chops off
chickens' heads is my favorite
joan didion character

I have nothing against chickens

this well-bred lady swings
her axe without a flinch
                    even as blood spurts on her legs
the way I feel at mastering a suburban male
who'll never understand
why I keep my floors and walls
completely bare

surrogates of archaeology

your fingers probe artifacts   facsimiles all
the way they do my pectoral and reworked covering
once the lights have shut their eyes
for the night   freeing you from doing the same

you imagine the body
molding under your shape
real as hieroglyphs chiseled on original stone

your tarp-lined curtains hold out day

when hens go mad

rooster after rooster after rooster
parades past my house
headed toward a vacant lot
near the end of the street

i watch them strut by   single file
tails shoved high
    talons glinting like raindrops
    falling through sunshine

none come back

the only thing i see
down where they've gone
is a fiercely territorial hen

guarding a yard full of nests
pieced together from feathers and feet
    the chicks in each one
    exactly matching its colors

new pillows

the sound of a glass
crashing to the kitchen floor
woke me from fitful sleep
yesterday morning

i live alone
                        forgetting where i was
bare feet rubbed against thinning
sheets   a tear i hadn't noticed
the night before

nothing kept me from
slipping out the bedroom window
just that the pillow under my head
was new and comfortable

intended for the occasion

green plate special

by the time the english peas landed
on my plate   they'd been under the heat
lamp so long they looked like
tiny little scrotums

i didn't eat them
        i did enjoy playing with them

the hook still hurts

the man i finally
let catch me
threw me back

safari nights

he wrapped his arms around me
the way a baboon its young
pulling my head into fur and chest
flesh to ear
words in subtle bass
rumbling deep inside
a week of pause   on a plain
between two jungles

why the men don't stay

the smile shines bright
under eyes gone dim

what's ten lashes

our eighth-grade p e coach said to billy
"mister hopper   you're on the verge of becoming second-rate"

billy looked him in the eye   smiled pleasantly
deployed a measured tongue
"yes   and still a notch above you"

with cheese   extra salty

everyone called ralph   a successful
    if dubious stock trader
"the grits queen"
a taste for southern boys no good
at conjugating verbs

inside trader consigned to the heaven and hell of fate
a five-year sentence near the mecca of macon

conversations during intimacy   #5

    you got a girlfriend
no   just boyfriends   you
    girlfriend
great
    you don't want one
how often you see yours
    maybe once a month
what do you do in the meantime
    call you

ghost l'orange

brash noises tumble from the attic
pots and pans banging together

    hardly anything there
        a chest of old linens
        a stash of dirty magazines
        a life-size poster of julia child

respite

six-three   thirty-two   two-ten
parcel delivered
signature prolonged to beer

quiet company for a regular
man   wife at home

sometimes susan

susan was a moaner
she brought guys home
and filled the apartment
with unchecked sound effects
until the sun came up
they stumbled out of her room
with looks of bewildered satisfaction
and sore dicks
almost every one of them called back
sometimes susan let them have it
sometimes she told them
only if they spent a couple hours
with me first
some said ok

good housekeeper

the toddler stuck his fingers in the fan
sending bloody fragments
all over aunt sally's living room

"my god   child! i just had that carpet cleaned!"

helping the hand of fate

daddy had just picked out his headstone
      a handsome piece of black granite
when a twenty-foot obelisk of white marble
standing behind us toppled   crushed him

Mother straightened her hat
               and smile

hold the ketchup

a plate of spare ribs
snapped to life
on the table next to me
    coalescing into a posthumous carnivore
    that set upon the diner's fingers
    and cleaned them to the bone

hang five

the matching set
in the shark belly

minutes before midnight

rogue senses pound at my door
peer through windows
behind drunken slurs and big-lipped smiles

"come out! come out!"
they growl through whiskers
"it's waiting for you! the smell of skin!"

barricades crumble against hot breaths
rolling down my neck
my heart racing fast in pursuit of my brain
which has already left the station
the entirety of its rationale burned to a crisp
from the sparks flying off my heels
as i flee the sedate world
of baby lettuce and table wine

headlong   crotch-heavy
into a crowded cell of freedom and male

Sergeant

i don't give a hoot about the melees
in haiti or croatia or somalia
people have been beating up on each other
since they were pre-monkeys

no sleep lost

just lying awake nights
wondering if the guy i met at wendy's

    he ordered a double cheeseburger
      and dripped ketchup on camouflage
    which i jumped to help him salvage
    under his smile

will need my service again

never on time

    the behavior of those
    trying to create an image
of importance for themselves

uterus envy

for the price of a baby
i could have a month in maui
a new four-wheel drive
   a table in vegas

for the price of a baby
i could forsake my past
splurge on the present
   scheme for the future

if i were a woman
i'd have a baby
i'd have a baby
then do it again

beauty school valedictorian

he had pubic hair
   the color of autumn leaves
      and it changed with the seasons

he blew bubbles

three heavy-set   hirsute guys
sitting in the jacuzzi next door
whistled lewdly when they caught sight
of my rear profile
      long blonde hair teasing my ass

i whirled   looked straight at them

"shit! it's a dude!"
two cried with as much disgust as necessary
to retain their machismo

number three lapsed into an open-mouthed
stare before a sudden weight
pulled him under

precipitate

men and snowflakes
    most beautiful
        on the way down

17 09

you pull slick saws along my spine
smoothly severing any serenity left
by cooing the words once mine
into another's ear

i grasp for lovers

apple cores i toss aside
when they turn out
not to be you

threadbare

so afraid
to burn bridges
you never get around
to building any

muscle alley

shameless raw flesh
held sister's attention
tight as mine
through the close-walled streets
of those humid island cities

liquid cinders

the beauty in the devil's eyes
as he drags them across this skin
lights fire to autumn prairie
thick with brittle brush
rough corneas
            scorching
a carcass kernel back to life
smoldering husk left behind

brush

redneck logic told me
to smile   be pleasant
i didn't know enough
to bother commenting

i saw your paintings the first time
a decade ago   in my head
before life   ripped to bare bone
left me no lull to beautify walls

you distill in texture
    the tautness of canvas securing your heart
then molt my skin
                with oil
                    with bristle

my most caustic of words
cannot erode   this carat of truth

traipsing toward two thousand

a bar full of shrieking sissy boys
watched a young lucy ride a broom
her celluloid bucket
sloshing a collective smile across our face
quicker than all the lubricated beefcake
jesuit jackoff clubs
and 1-900 calls to mother combined

shared secrets

implanting a writer at the core of your kindness
        foolish move
I wait   watch   everything recorded
your heart so easy to get at
    tortoise crossing the highway

        my mechanism of joy
        to see it in print

before the zipper is down

unless a freak show's involved
sex leaves me uninspired

    give me a pretty boy with perfect teeth
    my mind'll wander off to burger king
    before the zipper is down

give me a missing ball
    a stump of a thigh
        a question of gender
i won't quit till morning

asshole

anyone who doesn't do
what you want

boy did they scream!

the night of sister's
slumber party
i filled the bathtub
with snakes

my life

a fitful mess of slouching
from one conundrum to the next
most in bars

so far   at least
    not behind them

conversations during intimacy   #12

what's that on the sheets
dried cum
whose is it
don't remember

smoking rubber

last boyfriend fled for good
when he learned
i clean my teeth
and nails
with the same brush

sardine of love

portuguese fishermen
threw dripping nets
over my chastened hide

    tangling me in cords and mesh
    that minutes before
    had dragged a five-foot octopus
    up from a place
    he'd just as soon have stayed
    (especially if he'd known his fate
    as centerpiece on a Lisbon dinner table)

the scent of tentacles
strongly redolent of that
steaming off the four coarsened hands
and countless young muscles
grappling me low
on a sun-squalid deck

down   down   down
to a cool dark cabin

    the menu   release

god of the idahoes

they looked for russets in tandem
picking and fussing
picking and fussing
finding nothing but flaws
ultimately having to summon
the produce manager
a specimen so close to perfect
the pair of queens fell silent
and sighed

freud's banana republic

halloween
i dressed as josephine baker

    a skirt of bananas

by midnight
nothing but peels

day at the ball park

fourteen lips
>   one glory hole

sally struthers goes to jail

the offense wasn't that horrible
actually
>   just   at the wrong moment
>   at the wrong supermarket

her cellmates
>   a pickpocket
>   a debt dodger
>   a woman on her fifth charge
>   of raising chickens in her
>   back yard   within city limits

cackled at her   called her things
>   "blonde bubble"   "archie's cabbage patch pillow"
>   "miss hips"

when her lawyer finally showed up to spring her
>   they all asked for her autograph

engineered for daisy-chaining

the bare-chested young exec
crumbled to court when the basketball
caught him bull's-eye in gym shorts

eliciting from me
no empathy or glee

      just stark arousal at the image
      of what it means to be male

hard   penetrable

california

where the lights turn green
and the pedestrians
walk anyway

< 180 seconds

i was miffed at bob
    telling everyone we'd had an affair
when all that happened
was a one-time event
that beat an egg-timer

bob kept muttering
"it's me   it's not you   it's me   it's not you"

"no kidding"

leather night

rancid smoke   faux masculinity
    drift by on all sides
        transparent   by dawn

bitten in bed

Agnes hasn't had a bath in three months
          suits her fine
   robert's mad   a flea bit him last night
   i told him to crush it with his
   nails   go back to sleep
   not robert   he got up   sprayed
   the room   ripped off the sheets
   put on new ones
   ordered Agnes to the den

she growled at him on the way out

rubber toy

   conceived to give me
   what I want
   when I want it
   you trash your good
   for any caprice of mine
   backbone pliant as
   ropes of licorice

              the reason I kick you

to keep you

empty pot of questions

dead wattage collects into cold lesions on my skin
    numb
after-effect of fingers pared of electricity
    life terminated in   no forecastable end

serial killers and molested children
leave unresolvable spirits
beyond the clever interventions of lawyers
and priests

light used to dance and dry   some puckish
moroccan breeze among damp white linens

now it chances only the night
    quick   nervous   cockroach
    gifted at disappearing soon as suspected

sleep sputters   clammy   eggy
         under tongue
worth the effort only for the flying
    absorb the agitation   below   a moment
before i roll onto my back
    let the blues and whites advise my eyes

veil of dice

shifting eyes dangled adventure before me
the unstable kind that could either
plunge me into a night of new-found tendernesses
or end with a rope tightening round my neck

to a midnight brain
    the results indistinguishable

mathematician as a child

when Mother was a little boy
he memorized mom's cosmetic case
tried on high heels that were twice his feet
    wondered how the future would turn out

a stressless time

until he put on the frilly black bra
        a tenth wedding anniversary gift
from dad   paraded up and down
the subdivision cul-de-sac

after which several neighbors did call

till nothing but bones are left

a flock of wrinkling castro boys
    they'll never be men
is perched on that flaking doorstep
every time i walk past
    swapping the same old experience
      they've had   keep having
        circling   picking at it

hungry vultures feasting
on the last stains of roadkill
flapping away momentarily
   settling back in
beaks sharp   anxious
        smeared with dried offal

dogs don't care

the park where i walk the dogs
is characterized by wordless trysts
    and used condoms

i know the name
of most dogs that come there

not so their owners
wearing the leash of anonymity
every step of the way

obsession

not that i like you so much
      just   at the moment
you have no competition

family only

how dare you let some manic driver
dangle you between the stars
not allow me in the room
to look at your intubated body
now more like my own than my twin's

"not unless you're a relative sir"

your wife walks right in
    subtle woman of quick smiles

no tear in her eye

even she sometimes calls you
by my name

tubes and needles

him on the way out
trying to rake in comfort and pity
from anybody he could sucker

fulcrum of his life

same old clingy   campy bitch queen
he'd always been
now with looks and charm stripped
    down   to naked truth
so ugly not even the savage in his veins
could stifle the stones in my memory's hands

doggie style

my boy takes me to see
dog breeders at least once a month
knowing the sweet smell
of newborn puppies
makes me horny for days

brahma

dairies and bathhouses   the only place
i've seen you fit in
coarse senses rubbing against furry skins
as you milk the crowd
drive dumb beasts toward leaky troughs

feet   bare hooves   all the same
under your eyes

   i lift the lids near morning
   watch twitching pupils
   swallow   deflect light

      tight selfish balls of charred tin foil

hilton head

the bed was littered with lace
   he pushed aside
   to pull me down
the bride out shopping for shorts

fell in love with a cheap whore

a watermelon truck ran over me when i was five
nine tons   crushed nearly every bone in my body

came through it like a rubber chicken

now i've taken up with a cheap whore
charges twenty bucks a shot
     scars don't faze him   says he's seen worse
says he believes only the strong etc etc etc

he's got a third-grade education
knows what it's all about

guys like that are rare as lasting happiness
i keep coming back

he does only if i've got the money

skating around the rim of crazy

a gun on his person
didn't stop me

from going after what i wanted
or him letting me

conversations during intimacy   #9

    where were you tuesday
couldn't make it
    why
...busy
    busy how
my wife
    what about your wife
you know
    know what
the bedroom
    i see   well   how was it
not bad for a tuesday night

fetch!

lovers and dogs
pet them
feed them
take them hunting for game

pompano beach

as dirty bookstores go
this one was my favorite

glory holes   tight fit
big enough to crawl through

broken english

"i come this night?"
phones my father of three and papal format
a casual '¿tu quiéres?' disengaged from gringo smiles

my 'no' absorbed as fluidly as last week's 'si'

"the night of tomorrow ok?"

"si"

a coupling to ebb in pictures of boys
spun from seeds now shared on me

red cheeks

I've been considering
giving you a spanking

the only thing holding me back
                                I'm not given
                    to casual dispensations of pain

besides
I know there's nothing
you crave more

basic

you ask why i keep running
back to that blue-collar dick

the answer   dear boy
he knows what to do with it

beelzebub's ablution

I jerked his head level
with the fragranced two-ply
to enjoy his gushings of grace
for my earthly kindness
(coughs   sputters   ramifications
of our porcelain eucharist)

torching me to resume my clutch
on urinous tresses
an unpretty blonde-by-choice
incapable of knowing he praised himself
through mother's eyes

                              my chronic inspiration
to syringe his soul again

just don't leave a mess

"you ever think about suicide"
     boyfriend asked

"sure...yours"

token moments

behind latched doors
guys seek in bookstores
what their girls wouldn't give them
an hour earlier
transfixed by the magic of their own gender

answered without words

splashes on barnacled balls
    fitting finale to a night of words
    hurled with sniper precision
    at wispy egos
       shrapnel through cotton

now the ride is backwards
                  not our norm
nose still bleeding

nuts in turn

shy of midnight   the dogs
and i sit on kitchen floors   eat
unsalted cashews   a form of communion we
share frequently when sleep stays out all night

i hand each of us a nut
    producing a continuous cycle of crunch
a ritual you did nothing but ridicule
until the three of us decided
our worship was more essential than you

that you had to go

vestige

i turn it inside out
tongue along the ridges
the scent and texture
compounding effect

    the afterthought
rewrites the memory

broken dishes

better at commenting
on relationships than having one

they waved back

dark industrial streets
near china basin
weren't what i had in mind at sunsink

once the ball started rolling
there didn't seem any desire to stop it

not even when the cops
drove by and
      (the guy at my disposal
      leaning back in the passenger seat)
smiled and waved

testosterone pie

a trucker
                a buddy
        another case of brew

cotton candy

the check-out clerk picked up the
package of cotton swabs
        "you're not planning on sticking
        these in your ears   are you"

"no   but do you think they're ok
for problem foreskin"

conversations during intimacy   #22

　　where'd you say you're from
georgia
　　are you a racist
no
　　you sure
yes　　　my family's not that backwards
　　...you sure you're from georgia

negotiation

first night i picked up robert
he said "i charge"
i managed some disbelief
　　"how much"
　　"hundred dollars"
eighty in my wallet
　　"all i've got's a ten"
hesitation
　　　one am　　　freezing by daybreak
"that'll do"

pythagorus' easy chair

rectangles and rogue triangles
are tough fit

       turn them at trial-and-error positions
       top and side
       push them through   however possible

       keep an eye
       least resistance and maximum chaos
       are tenacious sirens

they want to fall apart

they want
   to get comfortable

food

to keep it coming
dogs try not to rise
above the intelligence
of their owners

oil slick

she took me to her bars
stopped
the men's grins
now focused on me

low maintenance

millionaire or ex-con

ex-con

tattoos last longer
than manicures

complex numbers

men and math problems
    rack my brain day and night
                sleep all but unheard of
until i figure them out

done   i lay them aside
get my hands on the next one

tramps and crazies riddle for years
the solid stable type maybe a day

throwware

all my goblets
are now plastic

    you dodged
    the glass ones

lunch break

monday depression had me call in sick
seek peace from the city and five guys
in less than an hour

office ranch hands straddling noon

mister streamer

he whipped it out   let it fly

        me having specifically stated
        i wasn't interested in that sort of thing

handcuffed to bedposts
rubber sheets beneath me
what could i do

the yawn of defeat
pried open my mouth

she doesn't leave messages

alligators populate the landscape
where i've ripped up my roots

    they hang in dark   stale waters
    with just eyes and nostrils
    above surface   waiting out of busy boredom
    for the next meal to happen by
    not letting summer's lethargy
    keep them from stuffing
    their sated bellies further

mother casts her lure
within their line of bite
hoping the black plastic worm
she's outfitted with two spring-action hooks
will snare the attention
of a large-mouth bass

wondering why
i haven't told her the real reason
i'm never at home to answer the phone

double knots

red sneakers on a tussle-haired father   late forty
oblivious to the conflict between
the grey in his beard and the youth on his feet

just awakened from an afternoon nap
threw on the first pair of shoes in sight
     not his
determined to beat the deadbolt at the hardware store

he caught my once-over
     fingers coaxing friction from granulated paper
pragmatism clicked in his eyes

a couple hours later
he leaned to put the shoes back on
     seated on the edge of the bed
          wrapping up his impromptu visit
               with small talk about the wife (at a conference)
                    and kids
                         (the divorced one back at home)
i recognized the smile and strings
from a month earlier

the hands at lace
those of a first-born son   a father as well

pampered bruises

he handled my body
with the bent of a boxer
priming a new bag

last year's model

his slow face won me over
   quick tongue tripped me up
a duo of car salesmen

one agreeing with everything i said
the other going in for the kill

flea

        i've got one pretty dog   one ugly   the ugly one's
blessed with brains   the pretty one's pretty
       the other night i found myself home with two guys
one a repeat   i don't believe in rules in these situations
which may explain why the dogs ended up with us
          three men   two dogs   not a big bed
       my ugly dog sidled up to me   almost falling off the
edge growled anytime the new guy got near me   she
didn't growl at the guy who'd been there before   didn't
smile at him either
       my pretty dog lay on her back   feet stuck straight in
the air on a tight spot she'd weaseled between the two guys
       snoozed away

rescue mission

four city women set out after the duck
leg broken from flying into the office window
       they crept close   broke into a run
        grabbing wildly as after-christmas shoppers
the bird hopped once
flew away

trap

the overpass dipped us in dark
momentarily   quick   sharp as a cat's hiss
intended more to keep a threat at bay
than lasting teeth marks

tarmac has always been your favorite surface
i know my skin is nowhere near that color

my thoughts often are
the way you dredge me up
to drop me down
before my eyes can fake dry

tracks of rat feet run across your face
and forehead in this dream
down along your   neck   back
leaving me to wonder which of your orifices
it emerged from and went back in

and where it's hiding now

cat's secret

fuzzy took to disappearing into the cane brake
four   five   times a day   tail down

"you keep out of there" mama warned
having seen me trail off after animals far too often
the freedoms and dangers of their worlds
more intriguing than my own
"probably just hunting for mice"

fuzzy grew fat   between visits to the brake
she slept long hours on the sofa
food desirable as dogs

end of july   she failed to show up
mama "snake probably got her"

mama stood frying morning bacon two weeks later
fuzzy rubbed at her ankles   meowed loudly
     back to her skinny wiry self

she avoided the brake after that
     occasionally we'd see her sitting
     about five feet from the perimeter
flicking her tail   staring in
               danger the victor

sanctuary

pecan trees were heavy with nuts
the fall carson   a wildcard third cousin once
removed and sixteen   came to live with us

on last bounce
    far as the state and family were concerned
a long list of progressions
stretching his curriculum vitae

all beauty   no brains

as lethal on a sly city street as
in a cottage on a farm
where sound doesn't carry

how to peel an orange

hire a servant

she made it home

the yard was full of peacocks
with plucked tail feathers
the afternoon bet got bit

an hour earlier   she'd been hanging around
eyes intense   tongue
precipitating saliva

grandma got tired of bet making the fowl
nervous   drove her off with a dust broom

the swamp was bet's refuge
free of grandmothers and temptations
that led to swinging brooms
anything that couldn't escape her speed
and jaws was hers

bet didn't whine or beg   she was her own
animal with no regard for creatures
who didn't carry their own

the one time she had puppies   two
she let no one touch them but me
        she brought the runt to me
in her mouth   placed him at my feet
nudged him toward me
    asking me to bring him back to life

i couldn't do it for him
i couldn't do it for her

wart hog

"don't let them spit in your eye"
dead ancestors warned   through
live ones   "you'll go blind"

i liked to collect them
by the bag full
easily a couple hundred a night

i had no plans for them   just
wanted to beat cousin's
record

                    never did

by the time i quit the evening
at least half were dead
suffocated

a boy's cache   rusted gold

last night

the young guy lying next to me this morning
knew nothing of my family history
or past ten years

I watched his chest rise   fall
    cake in the oven
dreams still peaceful

gator

he lay in the sun
toes spread wide
brown teeth sticking out
from under leathery lips

i tapped his tail lightly
    ran like a demon

he grunted

bowlegged cowboys

some are born that way
some come by it from long hours on horse-back
some get it from rickets

others   popularity in prison

the only boys alive

they smell with rot   teeth   skin   hair
odors no amount of brushing
or bathing can dissuade

i hold them close   head to toe
swab their breath and pores
against the grains of my nerve

hearing no complaint that i don't have
what they're losing

off duty

the driver the cop pulled over
had stopped me the week before

making do

you barreled out of the driveway
like you'd seen yourself in the mirror
one time too many   just missing
the neighbor's foot

your destination   the convenience store
on the corner   knows you for three things
        your love of cheap beer and cigarettes
        your tendency to be short on change
        a back pocket stuffed with items
            not listed on the receipt

denial doesn't stick as long as it used to

your skin still has the sweet taste
of fresh leather   eyes boil
on cue   briefly renewing
aging dew feeling the brunt
of an ascending sun

forty gone   i'm no longer the perfectionist

slap me around all you want

it's my fault   all my fault
i'm the one who did it
i'm the one who bent your fender
    caused you to break fake fingernails
when you grabbed   the steering wheel

please   don't yell
i get nervous when people yell
                        nervous and violent

i'd rather you hit me   that's right hit me
punch me dead-center in the belly
    whap me across the head   whatever you like
kick me in the balls
go ahead   i don't care

but   please   please   don't yell
i get very upset when people yell

at nine

demerol fading
      four times in one year
      had sanded away my resilience

i climbed the railing
limbs unsteady   tongue half numb

nobody noticed until the main door

i kept going   home twelve hundred miles away
chicago didn't speak my language
   the season march
decent grass a future suture

i dropped on thick snow
cold against bare buttock
fresh flake lighting on lip

in under a minute specimens in white
encircled my disfigure

they couldn't take me with a cloak of words

i let them take me with a shot of valium

the monkey boy

he hops treetop to treetop
the rest of us anchored in static clays

distance makes no difference
a meter or a mile   he covers it
more easily than us a step

we sear our eyes
on sun   he teases the periphery

no danger in him
plummeting to earth

     danger   is us
falling to sky

pretty men

macy's sells as many
size 13 stilettos as it does 7s

night at the zoo

the giraffe swung its head down
to inspect the child whimpering in your arms
    sun straight up

leaving me chance to verify profile
his curiosity keeping your attention from mine

       not that you would have noticed
some habitats offer less light   and face
than others

you ask why i picked Him

you're better looking
you have more money
He remembers my only first name

freaks

me thirteen and a sunrise
grandma began to check
the sheets each morning

eyes with nasty fire
switching to alarm

    an only grandson failing to spawn
    the sin she wanted to sniff

3-D

    you smile above   around me
your sideshow daring you not to do
    what you never would do by yourself

                I have your face

alone at night
    bulbs on my ceilings snuffed to the world
it does what I want

under the eyes of china berry trees

an el dorado with a louisiana license plate
    tail-end stuck in the ditch of a muddy dirt road
was enough to put a foot on the brake
at fourteen georgia farm boys
have driven half their lives

he didn't solicit help
    face   shirtless physique
    assured curiosity with kindness
    from the staunchest of strangers

i put aside the dainty of introductions
"we oughtta be able to pull that out with a chain"

one lay in the back of the truck
    i had no idea what to do with it
dealable   the county road bisected our property
    this business as much mine as anybody's

"sure'd appreciate it" tone friendly
        caveat unmistakable

i looked on as he fastened the chain ends
to the front of his vehicle   to the rear of mine
experience can't disguise itself   one easy try
back in ruts

he unhooked the chain   thanks

a muss to my hair
     face   red   from body acknowledge

he shifted to first
     released the clutch

          good-bye a wink

tobacco children

two white-oak snakes nearly six feet long
sprang at us when judy lifted the leaves
          coitus exposed   coitus interrupted

we made for the open door of the barn
     jumped into the yard   adrenalin speed

when the sunlight hit
they relinquished chase   slithered
toward darkness under the building
     us now daring the first
to go back in

judy wanted a second gun by summer end
i wanted a radio

daddy paid a penny a stick
     we had goofed off most the morning

time to pray

your eyes jerk away
   not because you see
      I want you-know-what

      you see I want
         you-don't-know-what

california straight men

compare pasta recipes
               shoulder to shoulder
at the company urinal

it cracked in half

tricks of all sorts
pass over my threshold
    tall ones   short ones   ones so drunk
    all they can do is fall asleep
my only criterion being
they not injure or steal

    after the last
    i'm applying a few more
a three-hundred-fifty pound beauty
proved too much to toilet

guinness pig

tom showed up
twelve bottles in the refrigerator

him gone
all were empty

two in me

a seven-set of mallards swims on the stream
through the park where the dogs run free
they keep their distance   though the dogs
are so terrified of any body
of water larger than a drinking bowl
they won't get within a foot

the pastrami sandwich i'd brought along
was from the supermarket the day before
i decided against it   so did the dogs
backing off from flea dip

i threw the sandwich into the water
the fowl scattered
soon reassembled   began to shred
the meat and bread
fighting over it till none was left

wilted lettuce lay in question
several chopped at it with serrated bills
spit it out after a taste

the opportunist let it float   unattended
     a school of water bugs collected
she scooped them up

eating moose

june opened her hand   palm up
revealing two items missing
three years   a gallstone that wasn't
mine   a fifth-generation silver
dollar worn too thin for value

she placed them on the table
between the meat and bowl of beans
thumped my head   laughed

the key to her cabin
lay deep   in my pocket

eagle dream

sight of hare
at five hundred

feet

wet cement

Agnes left tracks in a hurry
to get from one side of your
project to the other

i wouldn't have noticed
if you hadn't laughed   all i saw
was fur on your chest swirling
south   bristly as hers

how smooth your shift
           from dog to man

line of ashes

after the service
pour some onto the bar
take a snort

see why i always did
just what i wanted

camera sweat

skin and eyes   a tint
of orange   excess carrots
solid determination of a wrestler
to weigh in for a sport
that wouldn't escort him past college
            permanent images
in the wants of boys
straining our thighs to shoot him pin

Joe continued with his dying

    fifteen family members sardined the room
sister spoke

    a plane at the airport
    backs into a service truck   flips it
      scatters a whole load
    of in-flight meals   across the tarmac

"no one was hurt but all the passengers lost their lunches"

    whoops   cackles   doused the tension

    Joe gurgled   twitched
      ears already gone

crown of wheels

in wichita little queens
drive big trucks

in san francisco it's the other
way around

how can i compete

date with me
broken
for one with your brother

pampers

you insist on wearing diapers

    at forty

i insist you change them yourself

fat pussy on a power trip   grade 2

she sat on my chest
   flexing thighs
      teeth   eyes   unholy with sparkle

the other boys
fled for cover

plastic and pearls

disposable life
                    shiny syllables

blanket stealer

a wild burro snorted in my ear
half an hour before sun
waking me from sleep
           never too good to begin with

december in a bag   barren ground
above death   valley   trespassing again

the comforter lay at my side   bunched
    i reached to pull it back
       loosened the bolt
                    of a fox

tiny laughter

                    the sound
        as the fly
                dodged
                        my swatter

prick

you tell me i've got
such a cute bubble-butt

at my age
the helium is in your eyes

to the prince of the avant garde

the envelope you've been pushing
has long been opened

moo sick

a week in new york city
brings out the beauty
in a field of Cows

360°

a circle of twenty-two combatants   hands
folded in prayer
           the preface
to friday night outings

a moment of holy
between the locker room
               and battlefield

corporate re-engineering

replacing lugs with screws

no! you cannot come home with me!

why

i'll tell you

1   you've been standing there forty-five minutes talking so
     much about yourself that all i've had a chance to do is
     nod my head

2   for the last forty-four of those minutes you've been
     blowing smoke in my face even though i told you that i
     don't smoke and that i don't like smoke being blown in
     my face

3   so far   you've spoken at least fifty-four hundred words
     (let me do it for you   two words per second at sixty
     seconds per minute   2 x 60 x 45 = 5400)   and   as yet
     no two of those words have been in any combination i
     haven't heard at least fifty-four hundred times before

this little piggy...

"your fingers look like toes"
were words enough to convince me
not to solicit comments
on any other part of my body

renditions with butter

a tree falls on the roof
you call
"a branch scratched up the house"

i listen to how the park bench
waits for you daily
helping you feed pigeons
whose claws stay neat
from the pedicures of your vision

the feral truths of their feet
remain as unspoken as mine

he liked his back scratched

vacation on the florida gulf
kept me from talking with borax
a week

from knowing father
had sent him to butcher

picking an acre of okra

virginia moved yards ahead
always the best   the fastest

eileen and i lagged
    complaining about the heat
        the gnats   itching
how we'd move to the city
soon as we were legal

    Judy lay   poorly
another sudden daylight cold

Joy®

the depression has lifted
if all the dishes are clean

14 11

grandma pulled the air bladder
from the bass belly
    stretched it across the bottom
    of the white pan
       losing smile

last day i knew
as normal

drama

if only your breath
were as sweet
as your feet

breakfast on bethlehem beach

a slow wave broke a lesser morning
shells drifting a few millimeters one direction   then
the other   mostly remaining sedentary as appalachian
hill folk   the external and internal forces that got them there
rarely enough to pry them loose

danny offered cigarettes he knew i wouldn't smoke
his habit to filter all differences through a sieve
of politeness   the final result
        over a week of growing beards and impatience
more irritation than mediation

wind still as moor ponds   little danger of sand
working its way into biscuits on the blanket
a jar of deep-red strawberry jam   the anchor between us
looking wise and mature against pain   pink
skin   typical of almost-blondes
who'd never know much about shopping for clothes
that matches flesh gone bronze

danny screwed the lid back
metal-to-glass clack scarring the early silence
that incubated another sweltering day

he kicked off his sandals (talked me into
trying them on at a crowded discount store
two days before   though i wore a size smaller)   got up
loped to the ocean's edge   watched
water and horizon lap his toes
long   flat digits that had never mastered

the art of swimming   despite being born
with perfect webbing

7 pm

wrists begging for razors
                     not now
time for "wheel of fortune"

convenience store

jasper's neck sure was red
enough to put his pick-up truck to shame
       but not to keep him from spitting
"whut-choo starin' at"
when he caught my fixed iris
as he opened the door to load his six packs

         "perfection"

tense breath through tight teeth
      no witness in sight

"git in!"

meeting god

"you no-good motherfuckin' son of a bitch!"
he screamed   stepping out of his limousine
          white as hollywood teeth

"i was well into my second day of a much needed
vacation down on the coast when you
had to get yourself killed!
why couldn't you hold off for twelve
more short little days?   noooo   you
had to do it right now   you had to mess up
all my plans and records
and make these whiny four-eyed bastards
i have for assistants call me back just
to handle this   who do you think you are?
some privileged piece of
white-boy shit? huh? is that it? well
fuck you! and don't think you're gonna get
out of this so easy   no sir!
you inconsiderate chunk of rotten skunk liver
i'm sending you back!"

suicide poetry

          live to write about it
          you're doing something wrong

cosmetic

i don't like being around ugly people
i particularly dislike dining with them
when i eat   i like to look at pretty people
with pleasant expression
i like to imagine them on my plate
    served up with the startling glamour
of japanese food   in my bed
i want to lick their eyes
suck their toes
i want to wallow in their presence
    a dog in offal
i don't want to wallow in ugly people
i don't want them on me or anywhere near me
i like pretty people
because i am pretty
i'm very pretty

friday morning

call from Joe's sister
    he died last evening
monday   the doctors said he wouldn't make it
through the night
    he dragged it out   basking
in all the attention   same as always

Joe

replacing the bearings

beer   lube   hubcap

"what more could a man ask for" you say
with a sigh and burp among articles
from refrigerator   bedroom   wheel job

the bottom of the bottle gives up one last swallow
        carpet impressions and red fade on white

men who find enthusiasm in lugs and
putting them back on seek solace
in this room with nothing but a couch
old ceiling light fixture   thoughts
that entertain themselves

words of private life lose steam
between wellspring
and vocal cord

engines   drywall   grout
    those are the details that
work their way to the surface

your delicacy and decency
         to leave that untouched
appreciated

eleven minutes on third street

twenty miles of assessment with headlights
    taillights   eyes evaluating
mine through two pane of window

you know the answer to this exam
                        60 35 65 20 0
you know to let me pose the question

fate falls toward favor
    freeway exit with side-street parking

statistics are all i care about
twenty-seven   five-eleven   one-eighty-five
familiar zip code

the inches between us
excuse themselves to sit on the curb
until i call them back

don't tell me your name
i don't want to know your name

22 153

drippings from your pan
    better than a whole pot roast
        from anyone else's

sharp shooter

judy hasn't worn anything but jeans
    flannel shirts   hiking boots   for fifteen years

she plasters her hair
with spray before
vanishing into the woods
                a gun on her shoulder

                a deer in her thought

human

no one touches
the way i do   you say

dogs are good teachers

ginseng on the windowsill

an inexcusably wide and expensive
    view of midtown
    night lights soldering
    your belly to mine

tears me awake
no matter how many partitions of dreams
i erect in the way

dawn closer than dusk
i know better than reach
for the phone

unless it rings

wart

use all the compound w you want
i'll be growing on you again before long

rejection slip

inbred zebras have better lines than yours

fur

goats lying on the front porch
hold their place as i step over them
customary sniffs at my pant leg

never heard you raise your voice
        at them
you scratch the ear of one
    twiddle the tail of the other

neither skips a chew

            their luck in this life
      to dance with you
on all fours

clouds the shape of men

arms five miles long
to reach them

       hands   ready to grab

feathers and guts

"don't let yourself be tempted"
mother warns
dressing the quail
"it's easy for you   too easy"

blood on my palms
doesn't make me nauseous
or   heart beat faster

a blip on an urban screen
overloaded with blips
another quail skinned

fathers sit by the phone
hands wrung raw
praying for news from the night

illegal

last time i saw sri lanka
i was neither looking for it
nor running from it

it fell in my lap
like the ring-tailed lemur in madagascar
that bit my thumb   then scampered away
causing the locals to smile

my only recourse   to do the same

crash landing in the high desert

four days of famine   too many humans
i caught a lizard   bit off its tail
the only change   red in my mouth
taste   texture tolerable

acceptable tradeoff for
    the fat peace of being alone

ray

the hawk floats against clouds
   the color of cold fish scales
wing tips sharp as blades of bahia
pricking the small of my back

the sun lashes the mutilated citron beside me
cool aroma mixing with the salty beads on my tongue
foreign
as the shadow
that skirts my eyes

mary's day out

she threw mouths   eyes
into the air   one by one   snatched
from the beak   of one gull   by another

   some managing two at once

skimming the cream

your nineteenth-century tongue   a gift
for torching ears
even when you're a continent away

sharp-edged knack for conscripting
talk and technology as allies

        the rest of us turn into stiff paper
        blank on both sides and along the edges
        when you pop in

how you steal our words

yes   they do

i asked my brother-in-law
(as fine a specimen as you'll ever see)
why he smiles so smugly
when he catches other guys looking at him

"guys that other guys find attractive
are the ones women like the best"

white family talk

"but they're brown!"
sister's response when i told her
my boyfriend was mexican

   "including the parts
you'll never see"

he always got two gallons

rosie had the toughest udders i ever touched
the way daddy yanked at them day after day
mama said she felt for that cow
her face suggesting she knew more than words spoke

rosie wouldn't let anyone but daddy near her
she stood patiently   flicked her tail in obvious discomfort
emitted moans   sounds of someone
passing kidney stones   never walked away

she kept her head buried in the feed bucket
munched greedily   glanced back every now and then
to look at daddy   eyes glowing   and wild

tomato

ripe red ones rubbed all over
    juice squeezed on paper-cut tongue
      across poor eyes
cherry ones in armpit
    green ones between the leg
              jalapeños next

downsizing

they tell us to type faster
    as they chop off
      our fingers
one by one

abattoir

mama sent a case of pork rinds yesterday
not a birthday present   nobody in our family
gives birthday presents or thanksgiving feasts
     we don't put elbows on table
forearms and shirtsleeves might soil
     shirts cost money   i sent her flowers
mother's day   she called me   collect   said
never do it again   real estate's where money belongs
               good pork rinds
     peanuts   pecans   tomatoes
   are hard to find in supermarkets
mama does her own   she raises pigs on
fresh herbs and home-made tankage
     nothing from the feed store   when the animals
are large enough (shy short of full-grown)   she
slaughters   dresses them with old sharp
butcher knives   makes good use of every speck
of the anatomy   pennies unfrittered

sheep sleep

wool against my shaven legs

no bleats through the cricket drone
the night too dark to bare my shadow

high cheeks

such fine bone structure

I fantasize to see
        the skeleton clean

a man's world

    polish on my nails always matches
the liner under my eyes   but i refuse
to wear lipstick
    lipstick is for actors and sissies and women
who chase beauty in a tube
    if i could buy beauty in a tube   every room
in my house would be full of tubes as well as
sparkling-clean mirrors   at present
my mirrors are covered with meat-packing
paper or latex wall paint   except where
i once dragged a nail down
to catch a glimpse of myself
    the image jolting   a scar
on empress skin

the hesitant species

you stare through fish
from the other side of the aquarium
daughter on your pant leg
wife unaware of your softer scale

          a brush of forearm furs
the floor steals your eye

ozark caves

"hey boy! over here!"
i did as i was told   liked what i saw
matching swastikas on thick upper arms
bare-toothed dragon lurching at hair and navel

out-of-state bike and candor of physique
numbed my caution   lured me in
leaves of young hardwoods concealing my trail

gutted

a wide scar ran the length
of his rectus abdominis

terminus in fur just above the left leg
resembling the abandoned highway project
through the lower everglades
    a surveyor's mistake
        now a life-time of stares

thanksgiving eve

i could hear him coming a mile away
humming along with chrissie hynde
    that off-key drone that sprang smiles in us all
    including him   as he approached the last crossroad
before the lane to the farm   having given myself up
to the gift of my kin   to know the distant doings of those
who belong to us (most never aware)   their secrets
betrayed by the muted sounds sluicing through our heads

a rush   silence   stilled them all
    thick fog coalescing in a bottom

the trip he was taking was his alone

water the color of eyes

five   my cousin four
I tied him to the railroad tracks through father's farm
      no particular reason   I'd seen it done in the movies
and he let me do it   going along   as usual
with anything I said

I left him behind   at least one train
came along those tracks each day   he managed
to wiggle free   caught up with me by the pond
          at start of rumble

he didn't demand why I'd left him   just
scooped a tadpole from the water's edge
      examined it closely   yelled over the roar
"let's smash him! i want to see what he looks like inside!"

I watched tadpole   flinching tail seeming
to understand its predicament
better than did its dull black eyes

"put him back"

daylight joy slid off a
boyface
                    Tadpole swam

dog hangs her head

we were both looking on
from a distance
when the highway
took her brother

september son

he came straggling up the road
after a night of lowdown and high spirits on rat row
his belly full of booze and his head gone to seed
but still good enough to drive a tractor at dawn
the same morning mother warned
with a look of resignation in her eye
"watch your ways...the Devil's afoot today"
knowing i was ripe at the age when He comes a-knocking
before she sought respite in church and ladies
leaving me behind with idle thoughts in empty rooms
the echo of mantel clocks inching toward my prime
yearning for a taste of future wasted
within four walls   murmuring the name
                    of Daddy

donomito

an assortment of tools and other typically male
paraphernalia lay scattered across the rusty bed
    case of drill bits   roll of wire fence
    measuring tape   saw   two cans of nail and staple

red mud from hard rain a few days earlier
    much as a week before
had splattered   dried along the shell
around the tires   dull white exterior
    once bright   anemic   freckled

waist down   a mechanic's jump suit
    shoes visible   unlike the muscles and
ratchet wrench straining to loosen the worn
overly tightened oil pan pin

"hand me the ahm" he grunted   the metal parts
of the engine and chassis garbling his words further
    i knew from experience what he'd said

    his oil-smeared right hand appeared   ground level
closed around my fingers   grasped
without looking   the hammer

boots on my doorstep

I won't let the law inside my house
such do's and don't's and did's and didn't's

I won't let it in
and I won't let it get me
or put bars on my windows
or across my bed

I won't let the law inside my house
till it drops its rules and sweaty pants
and stares at itself in the bedroom mirror
the image stripped clean   free of its shackles

strobe light hooked to your butt

you light fires wherever you go
a pickup-truck redneck flicking
cigarettes on dry brush along
the road to any city
singing christmas carols at easter
a boy whose mother took all the credit

you let her   for life
knowing there's no point in trying to stop
others from sweating the flaws you wear
lightly as new year's hats

words from a hell's angel

that butt was made for fucking
    not some gentle screw
hold my beer   buddy
    while i pump that thing for you

priesthood

genuflections
under the sound
of zippers
going down

quitchurbitchin!

if the world were a perfect place
there'd be nothing to look forward to
once you're gone

immediately after the orgasm

men rush off
            to get the milk
          they're buying
        for their wives

over

ginger bloom on onyx floor
            vase   and   water
parting   ways

novices' luck

baby spider on first thread
into mouth of young robin

fresh
from mother's nest

shareware

to the lady walking her dog
   you hit on me
yesterday
   it was your husband

how to scare the middle class

be honest

glimpse at bears mating

lots of growling and howling
        gnawing and pawing
fur flying everywhere

                through

they put on leather
   head to the opera

first rule of poetry

truth
is for the twisting

spermicidal gel

in polite stores
often sold
as vaginal toothpaste

farticia

at the park she ate
two-week-old rib bones
left-over burritos
half the mole she mauled

    three hours of working like a dog

under the cover that night
she moved only one muscle

yuma motel

                        i got the last room
the others held by cancer patients
headed south of the border the next day
for an herbal cure

at six   the ridden wobbled   staggered
to the bus for dinner at a steak house
on the other side of town
            their ability to spend and eat yet intact
a few still looked robust
            most withered and brittle
parts of their bodies already
collecting as dust under their beds

some could die overnight
on rented sheets or from the heat they'd
endure the next day in a mexican hospice

the medical profession had long since
written them off   with me
            i would have gone with them
            only   i couldn't bear the way
their eyes scorched me with life

when men were women

they wore ruffles   lace
                    silly ornate shoes
ruled over moors
in coolish climes
held court and tea every afternoon
            nibbling dainty biscuits
            settled in gaudy chairs
        they had servants dress them
        cooks feed them
    they got their nails done twice a week
many had husbands

chamfered daikon

cut crosswise into medallions
a plate of ivory starfish
from buddha's soil

blue clouds

they're there   just not for our eyes
sly as sand dabs on ocean floor
   most people never notice them
till they see a plane vanish at point a
   appear a few moments later
   at point b

lipping

   "i must have blinked"
   "i must have blinked"
   "i must have blinked"

rules

refuge of those
who can't figure out
what else to do

gametes

when ovum and sperm meet
they become one

when sperm meet
they play judy and decorate

leaf sailing upward

pulled by unseen string

mary martin

intercepted

by a crow

level and out of kilter

four decades pressing uphill
to find my only wish
is to get off this plateau

note to mister cocky

i can't quote lord byron
    i can't remember the names
    of the last four presidents
                i'm useless at chess

careful   though

my intelligence hits home
when you're most counting on me
not having any

medusa mia

bap dee doodle on a two-tot chair
bap dee doodle where the sun don't care
snap me high   spin me low
bap dee doodle while i grow snake hair

cactus

occasionally i
take you for one
   so austere
      so prick   ly

when life goes awry from the start

you stay so busy shoring up the dam
there's never a breath to bathe the minnows

meaning of life

a glass of ice water
on a hot day

why i had to kill you

you looked back
on childhood with the fondest
of glee

i wanted nothing more
than put it behind me

how i became successful

started treating people
the way my dogs do me

jacksonville state pen

you went in for shooting the man
who tried to take your wife

you returned for the one
who replaced her

nature's revenge

beaches with no restrictions
on dogs seldom provide facilities

i sought relief in bushes
                my companions sniffing nearby

the limbs offered cover

        but not enough

to keep the canines from enjoying
a filling little lunch

pot of elephants

buy the pygmy kind
    the ones that have been deboned and freeze-dried
most good indian grocers carry them

uncooked they're about the size of a guinea pig
(without bones   there's not much to an elephant)
toss five or six into a five-gallon pot of water
    soak six hours
they plump up to the volume of a frying hen

add some rosemary   cumin   garlic   nutmeg
    any favorite spice   stew or bake
at medium-low four hours
    a tender elephant takes time

one per guest is plenty
to eat an elephant   cut it in half down the middle
    the way you would a baked potato
and turn it inside out as if half an orange

slip your index finger into one leg hole
                pinky into the other
pull the hide down over your hand
so that it fits snugly like a baseball mitt
    no fork or knife necessary
put the exposed flesh to your mouth
bite off a small piece (do not take large bites
        elephant swells unexpectedly
        in contact with human saliva)

chew thoroughly

it's best to eat the whole elephant in one meal
unlike turkey   freeze-dried elephant goes foul
quickly and is not good the next day

you need fresh elephant for that

midnight thirty

time   number
after six hours
in the bathhouse

how easily some fall

at least a year must pass
before i'll consider it

you swear love after only one date

sermon for every occasion

when colleagues leave a company
they usually receive a card   a gift
        a polite luncheon

our departmental evangelist got
a standing ovation

chocolate roses

pink ones picked at dawn
dipped twice in warm bittersweet
breakfast for a queen

to a cheap admirer

danielle steele is the one
who plans   plots   works hard

    poets   just hope there'll be
another one   that they can
make it out of the shower
before it's gone

interspecies

i stare into my dog's eyes

    the image of her lashes
    a miniature version of my face
    the bulb overhead

she stares back
lips tight

fishing for insults

his good looks   he said
  a mixture of italian   mexican
french   japanese

me
"an intercontinental orchid"

"how rude!"
    he stomped off

through white sheets

they'll be coming soon
    when   unknown
twirling toys of torture

stainless steel guarantees no rust
regardless time of day or malfunction

water gushes red
gold masked by ruby
a mere cheat
tugs-of-war not over

vane

before every action
you stick a wet finger in the air
    snicker at me
for not doing the same

so true of you
not to see
the one at your side

gust off the water

natural-born prostitute

god threw me under a large tire on a large vehicle
   pulverized my pelvis
      left my spleen in the biohazard bin

then he occluded my urethra   gave me bladder stones
   ten times   I didn't blink

not enough   he robbed me of proper puberty
turned me into a proper it   I kept going

punch   he weakened my kidneys   worsened my acne
curved my spine   drenched my bones with arthritis
   coyness faded a while   returned with the tenacity
of mildew in miami

a big miff
he yanked out my bladder   replaced it with a
hole in my side   I didn't care   hadn't been capable
of a natural piss in years anyway   I could still cover my
splendid little ass with a tight pair of jeans and draw eyes

including his
he made me allergic to most common elements
sliced out my prostate   allergies proved
annoying   not having a prostate
made no difference   I was back on the street soon as
I could get out of the hospital gown

suffer sassy!
middle age   major depressive disorder (the shrink adding

"you're one of the ten percent we don't know what
to do about")
wrinkles   gray hair   ice the cake

my phone now rings more than ever
men in search of spirit

god   give up

kindness

save it for those
who can't do better

sailing

i love nothing more

than to skate

fast

on thin ice

hear it

crack

behind me